Love Lost,

Life Found

8 PRACTICAL STEPS TO HEALING A BROKEN HEART

Robyn Baldwin

CONTENTS

Reviews

Acknowledgements

Foreword

[1] The End   1

[2] The Warning Signs   15

[3] Society, Social Media & My Brain   21

[4] My Happiness Project   29

[5]bTherapy   47

[6] Quotes & Self-Development   51

[7] Bucket Lists   69

[8] Trusting Your Gut & Truths   81

[9] Closing Thoughts   91

References   95

Dedicated to All Goody Two-Shoes who need to know that you don't need to seek out drama to be inspirational

Go confidently in the direction of your dreams. Live the life you've always imagined.

HENRY DAVID THOREAU

Reviews

My heart feels refilled in what my personal past left empty & my lone cry for help has been given the biggest hug in the world after reading **Love Lost, Life Found**. The rawness of Robyn's story brings a voice to the scars that addiction leaves on its victims, but also of the witnesses that are closest to an addict, even ones that are in love with them. She is transparent with exactly how a typical day was being in a co-dependent relationship, where even her "work/life harmony" (which she is mastering now), revolved around her fiancé's level of depression. Robyn wills herself to even recall the difficult parts of the relationship in order to create the exact image of how she kept herself prisoner in an unhealthy relationship. How she constantly numbed herself with the engraved image of her future wedding, only subscribing to societal beliefs she had known for being the order of life. She held onto this as a solution for their hardships & also her last hope that their love could heal his sick mind. In the midst of trying to love someone else to convince them to love themselves, her identity, schedule, & self care began to wither away, along with the relationship. But what happens when the happily ever after ends up being the rebuilding of her relationship with herself? She reacquaints herself with the girl that was forgotten, while also realizing that what may appear like a tragic time in her life, is actually a time where she discovered the true "Alpha Female" that she never knew was inside the whole time. Her journey through self-love reveals how painful it is to mourn the loss of a life envisioned. Robyn promotes self-love by literally giving the reader the own conversations & questions that were the most helpful to her in her process. She gave me the same opportunity to feel the waves of gratitude & peace that started to crash over her self-doubt. Her story inspires me to choose love, over fear.

-Em Haas

While reading this book, I had an inexorable urge to reach out and give the author, Robyn Baldwin, a virtual hug. Having myself gone through the painstaking process of reinventing who I believed I was versus who I felt society wanted me to be, I can relate to so many of the circumstances that Robyn outlines in her book.

Love Lost, Life Found is the unique and open perspective of a woman who was brave enough to share her very real, raw, no-holds-barred experience of ending a toxic relationship and the process by which she learned to persevere in a world that changed drastically from when her relationship began to when it ended.

This book is a must-read for anyone who has ever had to go through the tumultuous experience of a break-up. Not just any kind of break-up, but the kind of culmination that completely transforms everything that once defined the individual; even if that definition was flawed.

Although my personal journey of finding a new life after losing love differed from the author's, I felt immense gratitude and validation for being able to find common ground for my experiences. The similarities of the path to self-discovery were heartwarming and invoked both smiles and tears. At the very root of it all, we both had to take a step back in order to move forward with finding out who we were, learning to put ourselves first and knowing how to recognize the signs of a downward spiral when it exists. For any person, man or woman, when you lose sight of who you are in the confines of a relationship, you are not only hurting yourself, but all of those who want to support you during times of unrest.

Love Lost, Life Found is a step in the right direction to uncovering your happiness and fulfillment potential. Don't be afraid to put pen to paper and follow the path that Robyn outlines. Your path may not be perfect, but it will be yours to call your own, and you can find peace in knowing that there is no right or wrong way to heal a broken heart or find a lost soul.

- Amber Dunford

This totally could have been my story. Unlike Robyn, I actually went through with my marriage instead of listening to my gut early enough to walk away before. But I was too hung up on what everyone else would think of me cancelling my wedding and too hung up on my perfect timeline, even if it was the wrong guy. Just like Robyn, I had planned my life to involve being married by 23 and having kids by 25, which is why the line in Love Lost, Life Found that really resonated with me was " I was on a shortened timeline of trying to make marriage and motherhood happen. I would blindly ignore all the red flags in hopes that I could problem-solve around them and get what I thought on paper was the perfect life with this man." Every relationship I had been in from 16-25 was with the wrong type of men. I was cheated on, I was physically abused, mentally abused and emotionally abused. Even with friends and family I allowed myself to be mistreated. It took leaving my husband and having a solid year of growth after that to realize who I am, how my past and upbringing have played a role in my previous choices in different relationships and what I actually want in a relationship. I found it right away when I took down my walls and let the real me shine.

-Melissa Boufounos

Robyn hooks you into her world right away with her story. She provides an honest perspective on her experience rather than a fancy tagline to remind you that you are not alone with what you've dealt with. As women we have to remember to be there for each other and empower each other. Remind each other that we are strong, positive and fulfilled in everything we have, inside and outside. That's exactly what comes out of this book. Written with passion and honesty, I recommend this book to all women.

-Ayeesha Kanji

It's nice to know that everyone in all walks of life goes through this in some way. I felt like you were telling my story. I kept thinking as I was reading. I wish this book was around when I was going through my storm. Yesterday I was struggling with my own demons. I didn't want to get out of bed. I can tell you that your book and the great ideas of bucket lists got me out of bed. I feel empowered and ready to see the world with new eyes.

- Jessica Thompson

As a young woman who has also called off her engagement, I was excited to read Robyn's journey of losing love and finding life. As I made my way through the pages that painted a picture of the emotional journey she went through over the course of many years, I couldn't help but be blown away. This book totally surpassed my expectations and I would recommend it to all of the females in my life. Whether you've experienced a life-changing break up or not, this book is a must read for all women as Robyn's knowledge is powerful, inspiring, and truly provides women with the nudge we need to treat ourselves with compassion, love, and respect before anything else.

- Meg Doll

Acknowledgements

On August 25, 2015 (the anniversary of the date I was supposed to be married) I published a blog post titled "How to Heal After Cancelling Your Wedding." My mother asked me, "When are you going to make this date a positive one?" To which I announced "I'll publish my book on this date next year.

To Nadia, thank you for calling me an Alpha Female.

To Brad, thank you for helping me find adventure in my life, introducing me to my love of obstacle course racing and bucket list creating. Thank you for helping me define the first Alpha Female definition.

To BD, without this chapter in my life I wouldn't be where I am today. Thank you for your part in my journey.

To my parents for showing me what unconditional love means and ensuring that at the end of the day I wouldn't settle until I met the man who could truly love me.

To Mike, I unconditionally love you. I'm so grateful everyday that Havoc ran me over and opened my world to one with you in it. Thank you for choosing me, for building a life with me and helping me unpack hurt when it surfaces.

Foreword

We all have chapters in our lives. Some of them are "page turners" and some of them are "easy-breezy" reads. I never thought I would have a tough chapter in mine. I never thought that I would be a girl calling off her wedding one month before the big day. I never thought that I would allow myself to be disrespected by someone I believed loved me. I never thought that I would ignore bad "gut" signs just because I wanted to get married to meet societal expectations and live up to social media pressure. But here I am today, writing without embarrassment, and truly embracing what happened to me.

But what will you get out of this book?

I realized as I was writing that my happiness and healing journey boiled down to eight practical steps to finding a life that I love. So although I recount how I lost a love I take you through how I found my life again.

You'll discover how to start your happiness journey and take it one day at a time.
You'll explore why therapy can be a great healing tool.
You'll start thinking about how quotes can create aha moments in your life.

You'll see how self-help and self-development books can guide you.

You'll learn how to create seasonal bucket lists to help you live your life.

You'll learn how to truly trust your gut.

You'll explore what are your truths and how to speak them as you start dating again.

If this book were to help at least one other person learn to love themselves after a breakup or divorce, or to stop one young girl from allowing herself to be treated the way I was treated, then this book finds a purpose. If this book is only a highlight in time of how far I'm come in a healing life journey, to mark how strong I've become, then it will be my memoir, not only of a love lost, but a life found. At the end of the day these words were put to paper to celebrate the strength of character I've gained, enjoying an amazing life where I love myself first and live each day to the fullest.

The End

ALL I COULD HEAR on the other end of the phone was deep breathing. My words came out slowly and shakily. "Do you need me to come home?" He answered with such a tiny voice that I knew immediately I needed to get back to the condo faster than humanly possible. I was half dressed, hair wet, clothes and makeup strewn all over the gym bench. I can't even remember if I threw on my sweaty gym tank top or fresh clothes. Hair was thrown into a messy bun. I tossed everything into my gym bag and called a cab as I ran out of the building. I was hyperventilating the whole time, unable to catch my breath. I texted him to hold on: "Just wait for me."

I was engaged to and living with a deeply depressed man. I had never known anyone with a mental illness before. I had no idea what I should do. I sat in the cab holding my blackberry in one hand and staring at the engagement ring on my left hand; praying that the man I loved and cared for would not do anything drastic. I have no idea how my bones knew that something was wrong, but I could feel it in my entire body down to the soles of my feet.

Upon arrival at my condo, I rushed inside, barely managing to pay the cab driver, and ran up the stairs not waiting for the elevator. He was still in bed. Lying on his side, curled up in the fetal position holding his blackberry. I crawled into bed to hold him and tell him everything was okay. I was home now. My mind was reeling. I had no idea what was going on. His moodiness had never been this bad. Sometimes he took time off work and played video games all day. Sometimes he just sat and stared at his phone and played different games on it. I had nicknamed the moods, his monthly PMS. I had never seen him curled up like a newborn child unable to function. And then my world felt like it was crashing around me. He handed me his blackberry.

On the screen was a suicide note. I read words that told me that the only reason why he was still alive was because of me. I felt the weight of the world placed on my shoulders. I was now responsible for another human being's life. He asked in the note, if anything should happen to him in the future, to give his half brother everything that he owned. The breath in my lungs literally got sucked out of my chest. I lay frozen beside him. I read about how he wanted to end his life; that if he could, he would just walk to the subway station and it would all be over.

I didn't know what to do next. I couldn't function for what seemed like an eternity. It was probably only five minutes before I moved. I called in sick with a family emergency to his boss and mine. I proceeded to just hold him and cry silently into the pillow, feeling completely lost and overwhelmed. In my next moment of panic I remember texting his best friend. I was terrified that if he actually wanted to do something I wasn't going to be physically strong enough to stop him. His friend was confused about what was happening, but said he'd keep his phone by his side in case I needed him. I cannot remember what happened the rest of the day. It's wiped from my memory. All I know is I just held him and prayed and hoped that my touch would be enough to make him feel alright.

I had no clue that eleven months before, when I said, "Yes I will marry you," I was promising eternity to a man I now realized was deeply depressed. During the next few days he began to tell me that this wasn't the first time he had wanted to end his life. He had been hospitalized as a teenager and in his early twenties. I listened to him recount times he had tried to kill himself before; how his mother had got him to the hospital in time, but after, had never sought out professional help. I sat in disbelief that I truly didn't know anything about this man that I had promised to marry. I was in shock.

Two weeks later, at the start of a new workweek, I was asked to meet with my boss at 5pm. When I walked into the room I saw a person from HR sitting there. I was told they were downsizing my role at the agency and that they would call a cab to take me home. For the second time that month my world came crashing down around me. My immediate reaction was hurt and anger. Panic-filled thoughts started swirling in my head. How will I pay for a wedding? How will I pay for living? I was the main breadwinner in our household. How will we pay for the mortgage, condo fees or utilities? How will this affect his depression? I was so lost in ensuring the future would be secure, I wasn't functioning in the present. I signed a severance agreement. I signed it just so I could take care of finances for the next few months while beginning to look for a new job. At the end of the day I realized I had received a blessing. My fiancé had not gone back to work yet. He had asked to be put on a short-term leave-of-absence. The past two weeks had been a blur. I had been terrified to leave the house and go to work and leave him alone. I rushed home every night after work, instead of going to the gym or out with friends, to make sure he had made it through the day. I could now be at home the entire time and take care of him. I felt like it was a blessing in disguise.

I urged my fiancé to get help. I made appointments with a cognitive therapist and a psychologist to see if we could get a diagnosis on what we were dealing with. My fiancé was so uncommunicative during the sessions that they weren't able to get anything from him. I described how he would sit for hours on the couch staring at the tv or playing games on his phone all night in bed beside me. One therapist told us that he just needed to read the book Mind over Mood. I was so frustrated! How was I supposed to get a man who stares into space during "lows" to pick up a book and read? We were even told at one appointment that he seemed fine. I wanted to yell. Since I couldn't get him to come to an appointment during a "low," they never saw what I saw at home.

I finally realized I had no business trying to help my fiancé if he didn't want to be helped. I was throwing all my energy into trying to fix him. I was cooking healthy meals. I was asking him what he wanted to do. I started bending every which way to make him happy. His actions spoke louder than words when he started leaving the house again and going out for "boys' nights".

He went back to work two months after the suicide note and loss of my job. This was also eight months before our wedding. I was hopeful that he had pulled himself together and was going to start helping out again, while I took the month to look for work.

I had just started a new job at the beginning of the next month when my world crashed around me again. I got a phone call from him in the morning. "I have chlamydia". My gut screamed a warning. However, since I was already walking on eggshells, I didn't want anything I did or said to be a cause for throwing him into a low. So I responded, "I'm sure it's something you may just have had for four years that lay dormant, and now you're symptomatic? Right?" I rushed to my doctor. Thankfully, I was clean. My brain screamed for one second: YOUR FIANCÉ IS CHEATING ON YOU. But I explained it away and kept pushing towards the wedding date.

The wedding became a band-aid for our problems. If we could just get to the wedding we'd be happy. If we could just get to the wedding it would be something he could celebrate. If we could just get to the wedding it would be a bright moment in his life. If we could just get to the wedding our life together would begin anew. I was completely lost in the nightmare of circumstances.

In the following months leading up to the wedding our lives and relationship slowly but steadily unraveled. In May, he tried calling off the wedding in a random conversation we were having. With the summer months upon us he had started partying frequently again. His nights out had dwindled off in our years together, but had now become a more frequent part of his life in the months after the suicide note. In June, he mentioned how stressful wedding planning was despite not being involved in the slightest. In July, an ex-boyfriend of mine, who was in Toronto for a few months, contacted me and invited me to have dinner with him to catch up. We had a positive relationship and I confided in him that I was very stressed dealing with my fiancé's depression. He shared with me that, when his wife experienced postpartum depression after the birth of their child, he had urged her to get help and try medication. Based on his experience he advised that it would be more beneficial to try getting medication for him than to continue the way we were.

I was at work when my fiancé found out that I had discussed his depression with my friend. He was at home battling another depression low when he found the Facebook chats with my friend on my computer. He was furious. I endured yelling and screaming over the phone as he told me I had no right sharing his mental illness with someone else, especially someone from my past. He left the condo in a rage. He cut all communication. Since I had no idea where he had gone, I called all his friends in a panic, but no one would tell me where he was.

A week later his best friend told me he was staying with him. It was days before my 30th birthday and almost a month before we were supposed to be married. I went to his friend's condo and we discussed my "emotional cheating." My fiancé told me he could never trust me again. I apologized profusely and tried to explain how lost I felt when he was so deeply depressed. After hours of talking I suggested we put the wedding on hold so we could discuss our problems and really focus on our relationship first and foremost. I told him that I believed unconditional love had to be the basis of our relationship if our trust issues were to be resolved. We discussed that he needed help with his depression before we could get married, have a wedding and start a life together.

The first thing I had to do was put the wedding on hold. That really translated into calling off the wedding, but using a softer term softened the disappointment. I had no idea where to start. Thankfully my mother had rushed to my side. I googled how to cancel a wedding. I got my wedding planning spreadsheet out and started going down my checklist of things to do, working backwards. I called the venue, then the caterer. I cancelled the DJ and cupcakes. I called the photographer, who had become a friend, cried, and let her know she had an extra day of the summer back for herself. I emailed the florist and cancelled the order. I cancelled the hair and makeup appointments, the limos, the hotel rooms. I put bottles, straws and wedding favors on Kijiji. I sold them to a happy bride who came to pick them up the following week.

The hardest part was getting a call from the dress store to come in for my final fitting. My mom hadn't yet seen me in my dress. To keep up a happy facade, I tried on the dress to ensure it fit, pretending that I was still getting married, so I wouldn't have to explain why I was just picking it up and leaving. They didn't understand why I didn't want it pressed. My mom and I walked out of the store and I broke down in tears in the car because I didn't know if I'd ever get to wear it.

I couldn't find a blog post or an article that could tell me how it would feel drafting the email that went to all the guests. I found sample templates online that allowed me to craft an email that said we were postponing the wedding as we worked through problems. No website or online article could tell me I'd feel embarrassment and shame. There was no online guru that would explain how to deal with those feelings. No one could tell me that curling up beside my mom on the sofa bed in my condo and crying for a week was how I'd grieve and that I'd need to feel the depth of the sadness.

Since both the emails to the guests and to the vendors said we were postponing the wedding while we worked through some issues, I actually was hopeful we might re-plan it. I was still in denial about how bad things were and would get. I gave my fiancé an ultimatum. He could choose to come back and live with me again if he did two things. I asked him to stop drinking and to seek professional and medical help. He chose to come home on August 1, 2012 (just two weeks after we had postponed the wedding).

For the rest of the month he came home drunk every single night. I would find him on the floor of the hallway of the condo some nights. I would get him up on the bed or the couch with difficulty. I didn't talk to him or see him sober once that entire month. He never came home at a decent hour. It was always in the middle of the night. He was mean and belligerent. Looking back I actually have no idea how I slept, not knowing where he was or being awakened at 3 or 4am every morning with him coming home inebriated. One night it was so bad he came through the door, lay down on the floor and started screaming at me.

You disgust me.

Those three words were my breaking point. Those three words out of his mouth caused me to inhale and say, "I need you to leave tonight". Those three words let me know I could let go of trying to fix something so broken and unsalvageable that I just needed to pick myself up off the floor and say enough is enough.

I didn't leave the relationship because of the many warning signs and red flags I had seen in our relationship. It wasn't the abuse of alcohol or the postponing of a wedding. It wasn't the fact that I couldn't fix another person's mental illness because he didn't want to help himself. It was three simple words that made me realize that he took many of his indiscretions and directed them at me.

The end came when I realized I had spent countless days sacrificing my happiness for his well-being and that he didn't respect me or himself. That was my turning point. I don't remember how I even gained the courage to ask him to leave. I remember him saying, "I'll be gone by the weekend." It was a Monday night, it was 2 in the morning and he was drunk. He had been drunk every single day for a month. I couldn't even remember what he was like sober. I was at my wits end. I was sick with unhappiness. I found courage within me that I didn't know I had and I said, "No, I need you to leave now". And then everything became a blur.

The end of our relationship was nothing short of dramatic. Things were thrown; an attempt was made to rip the engagement ring off of my finger. Words were uttered that were so horrible that to this day I've blocked them out and can't recall the exact ones he used. My tears started to flow. I locked myself in the bathroom and I called two friends and his mother. They came immediately. I couldn't believe that my world fell apart at 2am on August 21st. It was four days before the day we were supposed to be married. That August 25th date still loomed in front of us. I was in shock that everything had changed so dramatically. Instead of sleepless nights from wedding jitters excitement, I was in my living room listening to him spout harsh things about me while he started throwing some of his things into one of my suitcases. I began to be uneasy about what he was taking, but was urged by my friends to stay put. All I could sense that night was complete bitterness and hatred. There was no way to calm him down and have a rational conversation.

I remember sitting with my two friends in utter disbelief. I was embarrassed that they had just witnessed my life falling apart. However, I was comforted by their presence as they calmly talked me into some sort of composure. I went to bed at 4am and woke up in a daze at 7am. I called my workplace, ashamed that I would have to take another sick day.

My healing journey began when my mother and I decided to go on my "honeymoon" together. We spent a lovely week in Turks & Caicos. I warned the swanky, romantic hotel via email that the trip was no longer a honeymoon. Upon arrival, however, I was asked at reception, "How is the lovely couple?" I nodded to my mom and said, "My mother and I are doing well". The front desk staff looked up confused and I had to say out loud, "I emailed the hotel in advance that this was no longer a honeymoon". We were shown to our upgraded ocean-view suite. I made jokes that if we walked into a room with rose petals I was going to cry. Of course, the first thing I would see was a bottle of champagne on ice and rose petals strewn on the bed. My mom quickly swept the rose petals into the garbage, and we chugged the champagne as fast as we could.

We spent the week following a routine. I'd get up first thing and go for a run on the beach. We'd have breakfast, grab books, a spot by the pool, and spend the morning reading. We bought groceries at the beginning of the week and had salads together on our balcony for lunch and head back to the pool for more reading and naps. We'd take taxis to different resorts for dinners of local fish and we'd curl up in bed reading or I'd curl up on the patio under the stars and just let the tears out. I still wasn't able to process anything, and was just caught up in a vortex of feelings of hurt and confusion about what really went wrong. I spent every night wondering what I could have done differently or better to fix the relationship.

I was lost in waves of over-analysis. Why didn't loving someone unconditionally salvage a relationship? What more could I have done to fix the relationship? Why did it fall apart so fast? Why couldn't he have just stopped drinking and sought professional help for the depression? Why couldn't I make him happy?

When I returned home from the trip I received two phone calls from his friends that gave me the closure I needed. They had watched on social media as my posts went from wedding countdown excitement to complete and utter silence. They watched as I posted from Turks & Caicos pictures of my mother and me as I tried to regain my sense of self and find some sort of happiness. Those two phone calls were factually informative and gave me a sense of peace. They confirmed everything my gut had been telling me for years. I was told details of infidelity with specific dates and times. His friends' words echoed in my head:

"He has been cheating on you for three years; you deserve better and you need to know so you can move on."

[2]

The Warning Signs

THERE WERE MANY SIGNS throughout our four years together that our relationship was flawed. I had moments when I thought, "What is going on here?" At the beginning of our relationship I should have seen big warning signs. These were moments I knew in my gut were wrong, but I chose to ignore them. There were several moments that stopped me in my tracks, sucked the breath out of me near the end of our relationship, and should have been full out red flags, like a bomb going off in my face, but I chose time after time to ignore them or rationalize them or justify them. Since we had many good moments over the course of our relationship, I was trying hard to hold onto those memories despite the bad.

In retrospect, I've tried to encapsulate moments of happiness that allowed me to celebrate the positives in our relationship, but I kept discovering memories of times when I deluded myself to think they were good in spite of the reality. Even the marriage proposal was surrounded by discouragement. The day he purchased the ring I got a call from my credit card company that my second card was being used to purchase a ring online. I knew he was about to propose with a ring that I had paid for.

I call myself an Alpha Female. When I met my ex-fiancé a former co-worker had called me an Alpha and the name just stuck. I started my blog on RobynBaldwin.com and developed the persona. As we started our relationship I was also defining what it meant to be an Alpha Female. It had nothing to do with being the leader of the pack or competitive with other women as the term is usually defined. For me it was about being competitive with myself, striving for better, and finding balance in my work and life everyday.

As my relationship was falling apart it was really hard to comprehend how an Alpha Female who is strong and ambitious could have a part of her life just fall apart. I share these relationship warning signs because I know now that the tendency is to ignore or rationalize them.

My relationship warning signs were:

1. "Boys' night" out at clubs that close at 2am, but he would come home at 4am.
2. Not coming home on some "boys' nights" and telling me he slept on a friend's couch.

3. Going away for "boys' weekends" and being unavailable by phone or by text.

4. Not wanting to tell me what bar or club he was at.

These were moments that I knew in every inch of my being were telegraphing danger, but I kept telling myself that if I acted controlling or argued, then I'd push him away. I was so focused on making him happy that I never wanted to set his depression off by being an argumentative or "nagging" female. I wanted to be that awesome girlfriend that let him have "boys' nights" all the time.

My relationship red flags were:

1. When we first started dating he informed me: "I have herpes". A visit to his doctor had just confirmed the diagnosis. I had no clue if he knew he had it or he had just found out. It was a hard decision, but I wanted love in my life so badly that I chose to say, "I am going to be okay with a stupid choice you made in the past to have unprotected sex that gave you an incurable disease; I'll be okay with it and we'll make it work." We chose to always be careful, and thankfully I did not leave the relationship with an unwanted gift. However, I knew in my gut the day he came home from the doctor's appointment that this was an indication that he did not treat his sexual health as sacred. Many people can change and make new life choices. I convinced myself that he loved me and would treat me with the utmost care.

2. Three years later another phone call announced, "I have chlamydia". Since I was willing to be with a partner who had herpes, the loving partner in me was willing to overlook a contracted STD that he got while he was my fiancé, just months before our future wedding. I was willing to say, "Oh, maybe you've had it all along and now it's flared up, just like when you found out you have herpes. Let's confirm with the doctor." The doctor slowly and hesitantly told me that was a possibility. I wish the doctor had yelled at me, "BUT HIGHLY UNLIKELY!" I chose to ignore this red flag. I supported him as he went on medication to treat it. Just go back to being clean and we'll be fine. Poof! Problem solved! I had blinders on and was ignoring massive red flags that should have any woman packing her bags. If I chose to ignore these things, how many other women sweep these signs under the rug just to keep up a facade of perfection.

3. I think my acceptance of his "need" to go out partying and not come home at a decent hour was most revealing that our relationship was based on lies and convenience for him. I chose to be the cool fiancée who didn't care about his need to go out drinking with his friends, and I allowed him to continue this behaviour for years. I tried to just be informed:

"Where are you going?" was met with "I don't need to tell you."

"When will you be home?" was met with "I'm going to stay at my friend's tonight" or "I'll be home after the bar closes".

Those nights that I woke up at 4am with an empty bed beside me were heart breaking. I knew instinctively each time that he wasn't being faithful to me.

Although the patterns and some red flags existed before his suicide note, I came to realize he used his depression to control his independence in our relationship. After the suicide note, I would walk on eggshells to ensure that I didn't set off his depression mood lows. I wouldn't say anything about the drinking and partying so that I wasn't a reason for a depression low. It got so bad near the end of the relationship that he would disappear for days on end. He just wouldn't come home for the weekend or a few days. I would call my girlfriends crying and frantic, but I wouldn't do anything about it. They pleaded with me, "Do you want this for the rest of your life?" He would come home eventually and I would be there with open arms welcoming him back. I call myself an assertive Alpha Female, but I couldn't and wouldn't speak up about his disrespect for me or for our relationship. I wanted love so badly in my life that I just allowed this behaviour to continue, hoping it would stop or change on its own. I tried to be more loving and more caring, which just seemed to push him to treat our relationship with disdain.

4. Before we met he had neither a job nor a credit card. I gave him a credit card for my account. I watched over the years as the balance grew with drinking charges from the

many bars he'd go to. He never offered to pay off the debt and I had to pay it off after our relationship ended. My kindness facilitated his abuse of my generosity.

The search for happiness and the "perfect life" found in mass and social media will make any sane, intelligent Alpha Female ignore the red flags and gut signs that stop us in our tracks - those feelings in the pit of the stomach that say, "This is not right." These signs are to be trusted. The moment your gut starts firing it's telling you something is not okay. Gut signs or intuition are based on a collection of beliefs, experiences, and memories that we've experienced in life. We may not have been in the exact situation, but our brains are able to recognize patterns and fire hormones that lead to an adrenaline rush or what is also nicknamed "fight or flight response".

Our body is sometimes so much smarter than our little hearts and brains.

On the other side of grief it's always easier to look back and see the lessons learned from a troubled relationship. My relationship with my ex-fiancé taught me how to trust my gut. It taught me to never sacrifice my happiness for another person's. I learned that I needed to really value myself before I could be happy in a relationship. I learned that it is our personal choice to be happy, and until we take care of ourselves we cannot be in a healthy inter-dependent relationship.

[3]

Society, Social Media & My Brain

I BELIEVE, I SUBCONSCIOUSLY and consciously allowed this time in my life to happen.

After calling off the wedding and the turmoil surrounding ending the relationship had subsided, I was lost. I was hurting. I was embarrassed. I was angry and I was immensely sad. I decided I would try therapy myself after trying so many times to get my ex-fiancé to consider it.

I've had three "AHA" moments over the course of several years and many therapy sessions that have allowed me to identify three reasons why I allowed the toxicity in my life. The first was realizing the societal pressures I had put on myself; the second was trying to portray a perfect life on social media; and the third was creating a subconscious thought that I could only be inspiring and motivating to others if I had a difficult time in my life.

The first part of the book paints a very grim picture. However, I want to make it very clear that through the grieving process I swiftly changed my thoughts from a victim mentality, where I viewed the whole storm as only my ex-fiancé's "fault," to one where I saw that I had actively participated in and allowed behaviour to happen or continue. It felt really enlightening to come to this realization. I can't put my finger on exactly when I started to think this way, but it has allowed me to understand how to implement forgiveness in my life - not only for how I was treated, but also learning to forgive myself for remaining within a relationship that didn't serve me or support me or bring me love.

This wasn't the first relationship in my life that had been filled with drama. Three times in my early twenties I had unknowingly dated men who were either married with children or involved with other women. In the latter case, this man ended the relationship with me when he found out his other partner was pregnant. I could probably over-analyze why this happened more than once, but I think simply I had become addicted to the feeling of being let down and persevering through it.

"Drama causes the pituitary gland and hypothalamus to secrete endorphins, which are the pain-suppressing and pleasure-inducing compounds, which heroin and other opiates mimic. Naturally, since drama uses the same mechanisms in the brain as opiates, people can easily become addicted to drama. Like any addiction, you build up a tolerance that continuously requires more to get the same neurochemical effect. In the case of drama, that means you need more and more crises to get the same thrill."

Psychologytoday.com

Why did I accept this type of love in my life? This led me to thoughts about a societal timeline I had adopted for myself.

SOCIETY

In grade eight, our home economics teacher had us design dream boxes. I believe that dream box created an unhealthy expectation for my life and placed a potentially unrealistic timeline in my head. She asked us to map out where we wanted to go to post-secondary school and what we wanted to do after it. It was a great exercise in dreaming and starting to think about what we wanted to do with our lives. I can't remember if she instructed us to map out marriage and kids or if that was my own doing, but on the roof of that shoe box / dream box in the timeline of my life, I was married by the age of 23 and had two babies by 25!

My parents met in University so I thought that was the expectation for my life as well. After several failed relationships in my early twenties, I met my ex-fiancé when I was 28. I latched on to him. In my mind, I was getting old! My original timeline had me married by 23 and babies by 25, yet here I was still single and still not a mother. With mass media and talk of when women should be having children I was now living with a timeline of the dreaded 30! I repeatedly heard that your eggs dry up in your thirties and there is risk of birth defects. I was, therefore, on a shortened timeline of trying to make marriage and motherhood happen. I would blindly ignore all the red flags in the hopes that I could problem-solve around them and get what I thought on paper was the perfect life with this man. I wanted so badly to be in the next phase of life because I thought this season of life was time bound by age. Watching all my girlfriends get engaged and married around me, I was determined to be among them even in the worst of circumstances. I wanted that dream box timeline so badly.

I was ambitious. I had graduated from my University business school with honours. I had been a CFL cheerleader for two different teams. I was climbing the corporate ladder in the advertising agency world. I was training and competing in fitness competitions. I was trying to establish myself as a fitness model. I was building up a personal brand and resume. I thought I could build a personal life as well.

I'm also confessing that I was susceptible to mass media exposure and mind shaping. I always joke that movies have shaped my career desires. When Free Willy came out I was in grade eight and immediately announced I was going to become a marine biologist. When Legally Blonde was released I wrote my LSATs and thought about a law career. Finally, What Women Want shaped my nine-year career in advertising. So it's easy to see that yet another media shaped my view of relationships. In University (2001 - 2005) I was on the Sex and the City kick. My friends and I would stay up late in our dorm rooms downloading episodes, buying the box sets, and watching scenes over and over again. Since the show ran from 1998 to 2004, I was growing into a young woman with the SATC women as role models, accepting their dysfunctional relationships as the norm.

SOCIAL MEDIA PRESSURE

Social media was ramping up at the same time as my relationship with my ex-fiancé. Here's a quick timeline: I got Facebook in 2007. I entered the relationship in 2009. I got engaged in 2011 and got Instagram in 2012. Since I was building a personal brand online as a fitness personality and an Alpha Female, I was sharing different aspects of my life with my online world. I was being authentic and as real as I could be. To do this I was sharing aspects of my personal life and relationship online. While I was trying to build a perfect life according to the image society had created in my head, I was also watching all these social media "friends" post pictures of their engagements and weddings and baby bumps as they started families. The picture of perfect lives portrayed on social media was exactly what I was trying to build in my life. I fed into it; within minutes of getting engaged in 2011 and telling my family and friends, I had posted to Twitter, "I said yes".

As the relationship started falling apart I had an image to uphold. I was a woman who appeared to have her life on track - the track society expected of me. I was trying to hold it together for the optics, because if I had to start over as a single woman, I was going to be "behind in life".

DIFFICULT TIME = INSPIRING

In addition to society and social media I had created an unhealthy subconscious way of thinking in my teenage years. I grew up in a Baptist Church. I was involved in the youth group, and I remember distinctly one night listening to a young man's testimony at a Baptism event. He shared how he had overcome drug and alcohol addiction and how he was led to a life with Christ. His words were beautiful, touching and impactful. I was the "goody two-shoes" back then. I had never gotten drunk or tried drugs; I couldn't relate to his story. Other teenagers asking questions surrounded him after the event and told him he was so inspiring. His story was impacting people who realized they could turn their life around no matter what they've been through. In therapy years later I recognized that I had asked myself this question: Did I need a difficult time in my life to be able to impact someone else's life and be inspiring?

I've come to realize that I created subconscious thoughts that I needed to have a tough storm in my life to be able to be more relatable and impactful in the world. If my ex-fiancé and I could go through a difficult chapter in our relationship and come out stronger on the other side, I could share that with others. I recognized that I had created the following thought process: Go through a storm in my life, survive storm, live to talk about it, and therefore be super inspirational. Now I recoil when someone tells me I'm inspiring, because my brain knows I had craved this. I'm gradually working through eliminating this unhealthy thought process.

I realize now, looking back, that I invited drama into my life because I was trying to follow an unrealistic societal timeline. I then tried to power through it so that I could problem-solve the bad into something inspiring. If my ex and I successfully pulled through the tough times and got married, then unconditional love would win over everything. It would win over mental illness, it would win over alcoholism, it would win over adultery, and I would have my perfect little family held together by love and faith that I could put on social media to show the world.

I find it fascinating how our thoughts are shaped and formed. I have learned to witness and watch my thoughts without judgment in order to understand how I created them, so that I can then appreciate if they serve me in a positive way or detrimental way now.

I cannot change my path or what led me to this point in time. I cannot change how my subconscious thoughts impacted my conscious thoughts. I can only educate myself and recognize what happened in my subconscious to see how I allowed my thoughts to become reality. I can acknowledge my actions so that I never repeat them in my life again. And I can take responsibility for my participation in a relationship that was not loving or caring or supportive - characteristics that I value and cherish and know now to be important in all my present and future romantic, friend or family-based relationships.

[4]

My Happiness Project

AFTER THE BREAKUP, I felt like I was starting back at the beginning, square one, back to the drawing board. I was awkward like a grade nine student trying to figure out how to ask a grade twelve to slow dance at the school dance. However you want to call it, I was trying to find my life again. I ate horribly during the break up. I drank a lot of wine. I cried a lot. I stopped posting things on social media. I had spent all this time sharing pictures from Pinterest of my perfect wedding on my social networks and then went into absolute silence. I stared at the wedding dress hanging in my closet and was overwhelmed.

I felt shame for failing to get married. I am a problem-solver. I pride myself on figuring out life or work problems, and swell with pride from compliments on a job well done. Achievement is my drug. But I had failed at fixing this relationship and was overwhelmed with shame. I had failed at saving the relationship and being able to say I fixed it and we got through this crisis, stronger together as a couple. I was still telling myself that unconditional love should have been enough. I was broken from these thoughts. I put a lot of responsibility on my shoulders.

I went through the motions of going to work. I cried silent tears at my desk and wiped them away with or without my coworkers' knowledge. I threw myself into my career and being the best advertising executive I could be. I threw myself into my side hustles and focused on being a blogger and brand ambassador. One month after the break up I traveled to Vegas to attend the Olympia (a massive body-building/fitness convention) with my supplement sponsor. It was perfect timing, because I was able to focus on fun work, connect with amazing athletes, develop life-long friendships, and just stay busy. But when I got back from the trip I found myself at a loss on what to do next. I thought being busy was the answer to ignoring emotions and not having to truly deal with them.

I really had no idea what to do or where to start on rebuilding my life. I use words like rebuilding, because I felt utterly broken from the experience. So I decided to put one foot in front of the other and started taking one day at a time and doing what I needed to smile and not break down in a puddle of tears. There is no prescription for how to get through a broken heart. You may have found this book because you were googling how to heal a broken heart and the subtitle is a catchy advertising slogan so that I could have a proper marketing plan built for this book. But in the end, I believe you have to do what feels right for yourself. The period of time from the moment I called off my wedding to the present day and beyond I call my happiness journey. I look back to the beginning of that journey and think, "Oh I could've done this differently" or "Wow I really didn't process my grief properly."

What's amazing about the word journey is that it's defined as the "act of traveling from one place to another". I have no destination in mind other than continually choosing to be happy and building a life that I absolutely love. As an adventurer who learned how to surf in Nicaragua and Dominican Republic I'm also a massive fan of the terminology around becoming a surfer of feelings. I believe when you experience any sort of grief you become a seasoned expert in surfing feelings. Different feelings can come and go at a moment's notice. Sometimes you catch the wave and ride that feeling out until it's white water hitting the sand and you come to a calm understanding of what you're feeling; and other times the waves slam you upside the head. They throw you off your board and you're left curled in a ball hoping the board doesn't smack you in the nose. You can't even begin to think about how to process the feeling you're experiencing and everything becomes overwhelming.

I came to terms with knowing that feelings would come and go and that I'd have to just take one day at a time. As larger and larger waves hit me I realized that I wasn't happy. I had always been a genuinely happy, smiling individual my whole life. I didn't comprehend how much I had relied on a relationship with a life partner and a big white party to bring me happiness. Thus came new feelings of shame for basing my happiness on another human being and society's view of a milestone in life.

I was also frustrated that I was feeling such intense feelings of grief. From the moment of our engagement to our breakup I had lived with pictures of a white tent lit up from the inside. I had pictured my family and friends snug in their seating chart arrangements and dancing the night away, myself in a white dress slow dancing with the man that I loved for our first dance. Throughout the last year of our relationship the ups and downs were so bad that I had held on to the happy pictures of our wedding, hoping they would hold together our relationship that was actually falling apart so badly. I was foolish to believe a party could save a relationship, hoping it would be a bright moment in our lives we could cherish.

However, the reality was that I was living with a significant other, who was dealing with depression, abusing alcohol, and was choosing to be with other women while engaged to me. He was not present in our relationship or even attempting to meet me half way in the concept of un-conditional love.

Now I believe I am an intelligent woman. I'm book smart. I've attended post secondary school so can call my-self educated; yet I still succumbed to a twisted view that societal pressure had put in my head. I really thought get-ting married would fix everything. After I came to my sens-es and ended the relationship, I knew I needed to "get happy" or "find my happy" fast (because that's how I roll), so that I didn't fall into a rabbit hole of self loathing and a deeper depression than I found myself in. I had allowed myself to be in this relationship. Since I chose not to play the victim and accepted that I allowed myself to participate in this relationship, I then was able to recognize that I would need to own my healing process. I needed to figure out what was going to simply bring me back to the happy person I knew myself to be. I didn't really know where to start. The concept of happy for me at this time was just to feel better, to not grieve or feel depressed, and to simply smile again.

I started with fitness and nutrition because that's what I knew best. I set easy goals I had done before to get me back to a baseline of health and feeling better. My first week, I implemented drinking two litres of water a day. The follow-ing week I ensured I got in three workouts at the gym. The next week, I tried to fit in four workouts a week until I built my gym routine back up to six days a week. Nutrition-wise I got back into the habit of meal planning and cut out any and all emotional eating. I allowed myself one treat meal a week, and that structure, which I had implemented back in 2009 when I was starting out on my fitness journey, helped me focus again. My energy was coming back; I was starting to sleep through the night. I was feeling healthy and I was starting to feel more like myself again.

While I focused on my fitness and nutrition, my brain decided I needed to move on as fast as possible in the relationship sector of life. At the time this meant I needed to date again ASAP. It wasn't the smartest thought that popped into my head, but as I have learned my brain has a mind of it's own and is going to do what it wants. In my head, I was telling myself that I had just wasted four years of my life with someone who was not right for me, and despite my efforts to "fix" it we had failed as a couple, I had failed as a fixer. I knew that I could be in a happy and loving relationship. I knew that someone who was loving and supportive and happy was out there for me. And I was determined to find him as soon as possible. I meant well, but I can look back and know I was trying to replace one relationship with another at Mach speed. The Alpha Female in me was fighting to have a perfect-looking life again.

I started dating one month after my ex-fiancé left my life. I was hell bent on finding someone new to be with. Although the relationship I jumped into at this time was flawed, it gave me clues about what I wanted and needed in my life. I discovered I could have fun again. I didn't even know I could be fun to be around. I discovered that I had truly put my life on hold for four years to "attempt" to make another human happy, missing out on fun and adventure during that time.

My very first, first-date post wedding cancellation was amazing. My date took me out to a restaurant where you ate in the dark. I shared my story about the cancelled wedding and the broken relationship and he kissed me in the dark. I look back on the fact that I blurted out my story to this stranger and cringe, but I felt cared for and supported because I needed to just connect with others and feel validated about what I had just gone through. We went to Canada's Wonderland for our second date and I laughed until my stomach hurt! I was having fun and pushing my comfort zones. We had similar athletic interests and he introduced me to the world of obstacle course racing. Even though we dated only briefly, he inspired my love of OCRs and adventures. When you hear the saying "every relationship teaches you something" I know that he taught me to push my comfort zones and seek fun and adventure.

However, when I started dating again I was riddled with anxiety. Thoughts of my ex and how he had treated me invaded all my thoughts. When I didn't receive an immediate text back, my thoughts ran rampant. "Does he not want to talk to me?" "Is he cheating on me?" "Is he dating other women?" It was bad. Plain and simple. I didn't realize I could name what I had as anxiety. I was still living in the past and anxious about the future.

Feeling as if I had missed out on so much life, I was trying to make up for lost time. Since I was so used to rushing home from work most days to spend time with my ex, I had given up all my passion hobbies. I had stopped going to the gym to ensure I was home as often as possible. On the other side of the relationship I was slowly realizing how much I had not done with my life during my years with him. As I discovered what it meant to have fun again my heart started feeling better.

During this time I also started diving into self-help books. The first book I picked up was **The Happiness Project** by Gretchen Rubin. The book taught me how to set goals again in my life to find "my happy." She encouraged readers to create theme months so we could tackle one aspect of life each month.

I thankfully read the book at the end of the fall of 2012, so I started fresh in January of 2013 with my themes. Here's how I laid them out:

January – 100% Energy - I wanted to get back to exercising and health basics like nutrition and water intake.
February – Make Room - I wanted to clean clutter from my life

March – No Comfort - I wanted to push myself out of my comfort zones

April – Strut Confidence - I wanted to prepare to compete in a fitness competition again

May – Run & Strength - I wanted to run a 5K and my first Tough Mudder, which is a mud run

June – Get Dirty, Get Pretty - I wanted to compete in another obstacle course race and do my first fitness competition since 2011

July – Soul Searching - I wanted to try new things and see how they made me feel

August – Date My Friends - I wanted to focus on my friendships and what I can offer others

September – Live Out Of A Backpack - I wanted to travel and be uncomfortable

October – Thankful - I wanted to focus on all the things that I've been grateful for throughout the year

November – Book Love - I wanted to write my first eBook

December – Random Acts of Love - I wanted to do things without telling people about them

After this exercise, the book asked us to identify our aims. Aims are a purpose or intention. To decipher what is an aim or an intention in your life you are asked to walk through and answer the following questions:

"What makes you feel good? What gives you joy, energy, and fun?"

What makes you feel bad? What brings you anger, guilt, boredom, and dread?

What makes you feel right? What values do you want your life to reflect?

How can you build an atmosphere of growth—where you learn, explore, build, teach, and help?"

Here is part of a blog post I composed at the end of 2012 as I was working through my grief and *The Happiness Project*:

What makes me feel good?
- Exercising once a day
- Drinking coffee in the morning and tea at night
- A great phone conversation catching up with a friend
- Cheesy text messages
- Reading quotes that touch me
- Finishing a challenging project at work
- Writing and publishing a blog
- Planning and going on a trip
- Laughing with girl friends until my stomach hurts
- Reading a great book
- Hugs from my family

What makes me feel bad?
- Losing touch with friends
- Feeling insecure about relationships
- Not drinking enough water

- Being late or unprepared for meetings
- Playing political games at work
- Eating dairy (oh but how I love cheese and ice cream!)
- Thinking of broken heart moments

What makes me feel right?
- Praying and doing a daily devotional
- Yoga
- I want my life to reflect giving, caring and loving principles
- Going for a great run
- I want my life to reflect a strong woman who is human but tackles challenges left, right and center
- I want my life to impact at least one person in a positive way

At that point I decided how I would build an atmosphere of growth in my life by focusing on what makes me feel right and what makes me feel good:

- I will build an atmosphere of growth by reading at least one new book a month that challenges me to learn and think.
- I will build an atmosphere of growth where my travel in the future pushes me out of my comfort zones to explore.
- I will build an atmosphere of growth where my words and actions only build others up.

- I will build an atmosphere of growth where I share my tips, tricks, knowledge and wisdom to teach others how to take control of health and fitness in their lives.
- I will build an atmosphere of growth where I try to help anyone that reaches out to me.

After writing down my aims I then created my "12 Commandments" for how I was going to live that year. These were and are the core values I would apply to my life in the next year to keep me on track. I still continue to follow them to this day. This exercise was that powerful for me.

They were as follows:

Be Robyn

Stop Overanalyzing & Being Insecure

Love Unconditionally

Smile At Strangers

Be Positive & Polite

Always Remember I'm Responsible For How I Feel

Why Do It Tomorrow When You Can Do It Today?

Step Out Of My Comfort Zones

Be Present

Be The Fun

Don't Keep Score

Be Specific About My Needs

And there was the making of my happiness journey...

I truly tried to show my ex-fiancé unconditional love while we were together. I thought the concept would hold our relationship together and bring us out on the other side of the storm stronger. I didn't realize that unconditional love must be understood and practiced by both parties for it to sustain a relationship. It was important for me moving forward to not abandon this relationship fundamental. I knew that it wasn't futile and if I still embraced the concept I would hopefully find that in others versus only showing it myself.

"Don't keep score" was a commandment I adopted directly from the author Gretchen Rubin. In relationships we can sometimes keep track of how much the other person does: whether it be financial contributions, chores around the house, doing nice things for the other or gifts. I wanted to adopt this commandment for my own based on a passage I read in her blog that spoke to me:

"It's meant to remind me not to keep score, not to stint on love and generosity, not to keep track of who's done what. This commandment is based on an observation by my spiritual master St. Therese of Lisieux: "When one loves, one does not calculate.""

Gretchenrubin.com

"Be Robyn" was the most difficult commandment to figure out. I had been there for someone else for so long I didn't know who I was anymore. I had developed a seriously unhealthy case of codependency I had to unlearn that. So I decided to try therapy to explore the concepts of dependency in a relationship and process the sadness I was experiencing.

Codependency is defined as the excessive emotional or psychological reliance on a partner. While interdependence is a mutually dependent relationship built by two autonomous partners. Interdependent couples care deeply for each other, desire closeness and oneness; however, they take responsibility for their own actions and feelings and contribute equally to the relationship.

I turned back to my personal brand to help me shape how autonomy needed to show up in my life. I had branded myself on my blog with two strong words that embodied strength and independence. But as an Alpha Female I was really lost on how to embody that in myself again.

I started by really defining what being an Alpha Female meant to me to help shape how I would live my life.

In 2009, I found the Urban Dictionary definition of Alpha Female: "A dominant or assertive woman, a woman boss, the leader among a group of females." I then wrote on my blog: "I believe that anyone can be an Alpha Female. It has nothing to do with being the leader of the pack or competitive with other women. It's about being competitive with yourself and striving for better and finding balance in your life everyday."

Then in November of 2012, I decided to write a short eBook called ***How To Live Like An Alpha Female*** where I elaborated and started my own definition:

An Alpha Female is a powerful and assertive woman. Her confidence is due to being an intelligent and intellectual problem-solver. Being an Alpha Female is a State of Mind based on choosing ambition and being proud of it. She strives for a happy and healthy work/life balance.

Type A Alpha Females often come across as strong willed and selfish. A true Alpha Female puts the needs of her friends, family, and coworkers first, without sacrificing her principles or dignity. An Alpha Female strives for synergy with the world around her. She wants a perfect work/life balance and is never complacent in nurturing the people in her life.

In 2015 I received several comments on my blog, that people just didn't understand why I called myself an Alpha Female. To inspire the words as something that was bigger than just me I started to feature amazing women on my blog, interviewing them on how they find work/life balance, and take care of themselves while going after their ambitions.

So in 2016, the definition has morphed yet again into:

An Alpha Female is a powerful and assertive woman. Her confidence is due to being an intelligent and intellectual problem-solver. Being an Alpha Female is a State of Mind based on choosing ambition and being proud of it. She strives for a happy and healthy work/life harmony [formerly balance].

Type A Alpha Females often come across as strong willed and selfish. When we stay true to our authentic selves and stay true to our mission we shine. A true Alpha Female puts the needs of herself first [I previously thought I always needed to put others first] without sacrificing her principles or dignity. She fills up her cup or puts the airplane mask on first so that she has enough energy for her friends, family, and coworkers. She strives for synergy with the world around her. She wants a perfect work/life harmony but knows that it requires being true to your priorities and what makes you happy. She is never complacent about striving for better and nurtures relationships with the people in her life.

You'll see that as I learned to truly embrace self-love and self-forgiveness the definition adapted from putting others first to putting myself first. I wanted to keep the portion of "striving for synergy with the world around me" because I did not want the ego to take over and make my life just all about me. The relationships in my life are of utmost importance to me and when you combine your efforts and actions with those around you, you can produce a total effect that is greater than the effort of just the individual. My family and friends mean the world to me; striving for synergy meant that I could take care of myself so that I could give more to others and thus amplify the relationships of those around me.

But going back to "Be Robyn" I realized that the most important part of starting my happiness journey was to truly discover who my authentic self really was. I would be selfish for the first time in a while because I owed that to myself. Putting myself first was the best thing I could do for myself as I chose health, fitness and self development, which led me into the next phase of healing that would reveal the self-love work I would need to do.

Here are some questions for you, to help you start your happiness and healing journey. Grab an old journal, a new one or even a scrap piece of paper and sit with your thoughts for a bit. I'll wait. See in you the next chapter.

HAPPINESS PROJECT JOURNAL SECTION

1. Grab a copy of The Happiness Project and carve out time to read it after this book if you feel drawn to it.

2. Start by figuring out your aims.

3. Devise monthly themes for your upcoming year starting with next month.

4. Write out your commandments somewhere you can see them. Store them on your phone or on a paper stuck to your fridge.

5. Define what Be ____ (Insert Your First Name Here) means to you. What characteristics about you do you absolutely love?

[5]

Therapy

I BELIEVE SEEING a therapist has been instrumental to my healing journey.

The only reason why I believe the cliché "Time heals all wounds" is even partly true is because over time we are given a chance to come into consciousness: to come into awareness of how our brain works, how it has affected our actions, and what we know to be true in our world.

After the relationship ended I started seeing a student therapist who was just finishing her psychotherapy degree. I saw her for several months as I started working through the hurt. At the time of the break up I didn't want to admit I was hurting. I didn't want to admit there was emotional pain. I tried desperately to bury it inside me and say I was stronger than tears. I hated crying in therapy. I still hate crying to a degree these days. I have always seen it as a sign of weakness instead of empowerment.

After my first session I asked my therapist what I should be getting out of it. She told me that it might simply be that I feel just a bit lighter after each session. This statement really stuck with me. I wasn't trying to solve my depression in one session. I wasn't trying to snap my fingers and get rid of the grief I was experiencing. I was simply just sharing my thoughts and feelings so I could feel lighter.

I didn't go for very long - only a few short months. I found that talking about pain wasn't always beneficial for me, and I wanted to focus on living again.

However, after dating for a few years and enduring two hurtful experiences that happened back to back in February and March of 2014, I decided that I needed to feel lighter again and process some negative thoughts I was having. I again returned to psychotherapy to figure out after these dating mishaps why I was being so hard on myself. After a gentleman told me he wanted to marry me and start a life with me while dating another woman (which I discovered on Instagram) and after another gentleman was so excited to start a relationship with me, said all the right things, had all the right actions, and then ghosted me to surface with a girlfriend on Facebook. I started asking myself really hard questions.

The questions, "Why am I not enough?", "Why won't they choose me?" kept replaying over and over again in my head after every breakup. I was so excited about commencing a relationship that I didn't stop to think if these were even the right relationships to be in. I wanted to build fast and furious relationships, because getting to know these guys was so much fun. There was excitement and passion and then the guy would disappear like he was Houdini. I didn't stop to think once that they weren't the right partners for me, or that I wasn't for them, or that it had nothing to do with my self worth.

The greatest gift from therapy for me has been talking to a third person without any judgment to work my thoughts out, verbally. I discovered what my "hurt buttons" are so that I can recognize them and understand the shame and embarrassment associated with them that will continue to surface over time, and how to deal with those emotions. I've learned that journaling is a beautiful tool that I can use constantly outside of sessions when I need to process thoughts or simply get them out of my brain.

Writing this book was first and foremost amazing therapy for me. There are just so many ways that the word therapy applies to different activities outside of sitting across from an educated individual, but in combination create an atmosphere for healing.

Here are some questions for you to process your thoughts. I'll wait. If you don't currently have a therapist or have an inkling of curiosity about therapy I urge you to find one and try a few sessions. It's like dating; you have to find the right fit.

THERAPY JOURNAL SECTION

1. Do you like talking things out with family or friends when you're trying to work out a problem?

2. Do you see crying or grief as a sign of weakness?

3. Are you curious to discover if your upbringing has created any subconscious thoughts that aren't serving you well?

4. Do you want to feel a bit lighter from the burdens you're shouldering?

5. Have you tried journaling to work through your thoughts and would appreciate the guidance of a professional?

[6]

Quotes & Self-Development

QUOTES FOR ME WERE and are another form of personal therapy. I see them as written words that can provide clarity or generational wisdom that "speak" to me in different ways. They help bring clarity to a thought that I'm trying to process or smack me upside the head with common sense that isn't so common in my brain. We read thoughts based on our personal experiences and see meaning based on what we've been through and based on answers we are seeking. During the first year after leaving the relationship I had horrible anxiety and insomnia. I would lie in bed awake with my thoughts swirling around in my head. They just wouldn't stop. I couldn't figure out how to turn off the switch. I constantly felt like "the crazy" going on inside my head was uncontrollable. So at times when I couldn't sleep I would turn to Pinterest. I opened the app on my phone, clicked on the search icon, found the quote category, and just started scrolling. I read every quote that would scroll by in my feed. I just started absorbing the words and trying to find meaning for the worry in my head.

I started seeing quotes that told me that what I had just gone through wasn't in vain.

> YOUR JOURNEY HAS MOLDED
> YOU FOR YOUR GREATER GOOD,
> AND IT WAS EXACTLY WHAT IT NEEDED TO BE.
> DON'T THINK THAT YOU'VE LOST TIME.
> IT TOOK EACH AND EVERY
> SITUATION YOU HAVE ENCOUNTERED
> TO BRING YOU TO THE NOW.
> AND NOW IS RIGHT ON TIME.

I found quotes that told me I was strong enough to endure.

I found quotes that told me I would grow from this grief.

I found quotes that told me that I just had to let things go and move on.

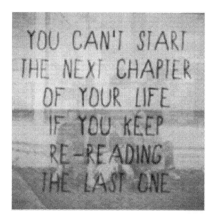

I found a quote by Lucille Ball that told me to "love yourself first and everything else falls into place".

Love yourself first and
everything else falls into line.
You really have to love yourself
to get anything done in this world.
Lucille Ball

As I discovered these quotes I sat up in my bed, tears streaming down my face and realized I didn't love myself. It dawned on me after reading that last quote that if I had let myself be treated so badly I must not value who I was as a human being. I had compromised my standards. I had settled for something less than ideal to appease society's view of what next steps I should take in life. Only a few short months after the break up I realized that before anything else I did in my healing journey I needed to teach myself to love myself again.

The definition of self-love is:

Regard for one's own well being and happiness (chiefly considered as a desirable rather than narcissistic characteristic)

or

The instinct by which one's actions are directed to the promotion of one's own welfare or well-being, especially an excessive regard for one's own advantage.

I knew what my personality was like at work. I knew what my personality was like with my family. And I had come to know what my personality was like in a relationship trying to please another person. But I didn't remember what my independent, fun-seeking, fun-loving Robyn looked like. She had been gone for a while. I needed to discover her all over again. I had changed so much in four years that I was having a hard time remembering what I was like. Since I called off the wedding, left the relationship, and started my happiness journey, I look back each year and am blown away at how much I change daily, weekly and monthly. I'm so very different now and I truly believe it's due to learning to embrace self-love, finding things that make me happy, being true to my aims, my 12 commandments and finding a life filled with self-love.

The concept of self-love was totally foreign to me until recently. I didn't understand the concept of loving myself before another. Self-love may be something you easily understand because you had to learn to love yourself early on in life due to different circumstances. For me personally, I grew up in a loving family unit. I grew up with the notion of a husband and wife unconditionally loving each other. Because I grew up seeing an amazing relationship between my parents, grandparents and aunts and uncles, I identified love with being in an amazing family. And that's what I tried to create with every inch of my being. When I walked out on the other side of the broken relationship I wasn't whole. I had become so focused on making another person happy that I barely knew what made me happy. I had a vague recollection, but I needed to rediscover it again.

When I sat down to write out my aims for **The Happiness Project** it was really easy to remember what I like doing. It was such a great time for introspection and walking down memory lane. Figuring out what I wanted to do more of in my life wasn't hard. The difficult part in the healing process was to understand how I felt about myself. I realized that in parallel I needed to forgive myself at the same time as finding the fun again.

I was really angry with myself. I had grown up in such a loving family and then allowed myself to accept less than amazing. In addition to the anger I felt guilty for working so tirelessly to fix something that was so flawed. I did not love the woman I had become. I was horrible at forgiving myself. Feelings of anger and un-forgiveness for myself created a great recipe for self-loathing and frustration.

I soon realized that two essential concepts I needed to embrace as I set out to find a life that I love were self-forgiveness and self-love all wrapped up into one.

One day I came across a couple of my friends on social media who were wearing these beautiful necklaces called malas. I googled malas and found the website for Tiny Devotions (tinydevotions.ca). I was drawn to a section of their website labeled Healing and clicked on the Rose Quartz Mala. As I started reading the description of this necklace I was inspired that this necklace was a symbol of what I needed. I was drawn to the sentence: this mala exudes nurturing vibrations promoting self-love.

Whenever I wore the mala I was reminded of the simple fact that I must learn to love myself again. I was reminded to be patient with myself. I was reminded to be gentle with myself. One day at a time I came back to the awesome realization that I was good. I spent a lifetime being an overachiever. I didn't need to overachieve at self-love. I just needed to say I forgive myself for anything I've previously chosen in my life that has led me to this moment. I learned to reframe all the negativity. I learned to forgive myself for all the feelings of self-dislike that I had let myself have in that relationship. I learned to forgive myself for trying so hard to fix it. I learned to flip negative thoughts into loving ones. I realized and understood that my soul was much stronger, and this relationship was meant to allow me to grow.

Surfing quotes on Pinterest also helped me to discover the hashtag #spiritjunkie, which led me to discover Gabrielle Bernstein's books **Spirit Junkie, Add More Ing to Your Life, May Cause Miracles** and **Miracles Now**. I started reading these books with a lot of embarrassment. I was saying things in my head like, "What kind of Alpha Female needs a self-help book?" Well I can easily answer that now. We all do, and I shout loudly from the top of rooftops how much I love self-help or self-development books. Self-development is a much easier term for Alpha Females to accept.

I really liked Gabby Bernstein. She was young and approachable. She had a large following of Spirit Junkies. They were strong women talking about her on social media and about what her books had done for them. I read **Spirit Junkie** first to understand her concepts, then **Add More Ing to Your Life** to understand her thoughts on spirituality and happiness. From there I read **May Cause Miracles**, which is a forty-day practical guide to changing our negative thoughts and perceiving the world anew.

I learned that the majority of my thoughts and anxiety were based on fear. I learned how to forgive myself and treat myself nicer. I learned self-compassion. We are so hard on ourselves at times that we forget we are our best ally. As women we are sometimes so critical of ourselves and just need to learn to love ourselves first before we can love another. This was yet another concept I was struggling with as I was trying to date and discover a new love in my life while still working on loving myself.

I forgive myself for choosing fear and today I choose love instead.

In many of my aimless Pinterest wanderings I also found strength quotes. I found ones that told me "strength will find you sooner than you ever thought".

In moments where quotes would speak to me in such an eye opening way I would breathe a deep sigh of relief and I would settle into a peaceful sleep. It wasn't a miraculous overnight change in my thoughts. It was a daily practice in changing my mindset from self-loathing, confusion and frustration to clarity, peace, and self-love. Reading quotes was a necessary redirection that I needed to be able to put anxious thoughts in a drawer for the night, shut it, and be able to sleep. For months it was something I needed to do every day. The actions of scrolling through quotes became a nightly therapy session of mind exploration.

And then some days I would read quotes that just knocked me upside the head and made me sit up with what I call my AHA moments. They were naturally just common sense statements, but I had become so blinded that I couldn't recognize the truth. Some quotes I would read and exclaim, "Wow that is such a life truth". Nothing was ever truly a new concept to me. There were so many different things that I knew to be true, but I just wasn't accepting them as truths in my life. Quotes allowed my brain to process concepts one at a time, when I was ready to actually read and absorb the words.

I then started to dive into relationship quotes such as, "You don't need someone to complete you. You only need someone to accept you completely".

These things made complete sense to me, but I hadn't been living my life this way. Some nights I would get angry for being such a highly intelligent woman that struggled so much to understand basic concepts when it came to what a healthy relationship might look like.

Quotes taught me to be okay with an apology I never got.

"LIFE BECOMES
EASIER WHEN YOU
LEARN TO ACCEPT
AN APOLOGY YOU
NEVER GOT."

-ROBERT BRAULT-

Quotes taught me to start to learn how to trust my gut.

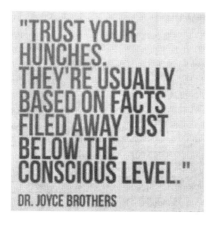

"TRUST YOUR
HUNCHES.
THEY'RE USUALLY
BASED ON FACTS
FILED AWAY JUST
BELOW THE
CONSCIOUS LEVEL."
DR. JOYCE BROTHERS

Quotes taught me how to deal with anxiety.

Be gentle with yourself, you're doing the best you can.

Quotes taught me it was okay to be upset - that I was allowed to have sad feelings and that "feelings are much like waves. We can't stop them from coming, but we can choose which one to surf".

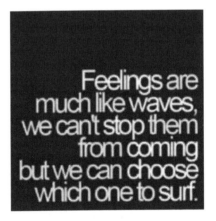

Feelings are much like waves, we can't stop them from coming but we can choose which one to surf.

I learned that it was okay to not be strong and actually feel a feeling, even the sad ones. I learned to let go of my need to be strong and stoic; to allow myself to truly cry, and to allow the hurt to wash over me so I could let it go out of my heart. To this day this is something I'm still learning!

I accepted that I would have good and bad days. I learned to be okay knowing that things like sights and sounds might trigger memories, and I was allowed to feel pain and then pick myself up and move on.

Seven months after we had left our relationship I received a text that my ex-fiancé was going to become a father. As I started to calculate the timing of the announcement, I realized that was a dangerous rabbit hole to go down. The exact timing was only going to potentially add to the hurt. When my friends found out they exclaimed loudly that I had dodged a massive bullet. Instead of relief, the news left me gutted and crying. Despite knowing that this was not the relationship for me, the image of a family being together and growing together just came over me and I was overcome yet again in my grief because that's all I had wanted to build in my life. Despite completely knowing that I wasn't supposed to have a family with this man, it still hurt to hear that it was happening for him.

Once again Pinterest quotes came to my rescue. They taught me forgiveness.

> FORGIVENESS DOESN'T
> EXCUSE THEIR BEHAVIOR.
>
> FORGIVENESS PREVENTS
> THEIR BEHAVIOR FROM
> DESTROYING YOUR HEART
>
> #BEYONDORDINARY

They taught me to remember I deserve so much more.

> You deserve the
> love you keep
> trying to give
> everyone else.

They reminded me that I deserve amazingness and not just society's status quo.

Quotes, paired with self-development books and diving into therapy allowed me to discover that I was in control of my healing journey. And so began and continues daily my journey of self-awareness, self-love, self-compassion, being present and letting go of life expectations, while still being a strong and ambitious Alpha Female.

Quotes and reading started to teach me that, after so much analysis of my brain and how I was wired, I needed to let go of my idea of future expectations and live in the present. This concept is so much easier said than done, so I picked up the book **The Power of Now** by Eckhart Tolle. This book started to reinforce quotes by him that I had found.

> Most humans are never fully present in the now, because unconsciously they believe that the next moment must be more important than this one. But then you miss your whole life, which is never *not* now. And that's a revelation for some people: to realize that your life is only ever now.
>
> Eckhart Tolle

I embraced self-help books and, as I dived back into the world of dating, I read **The 5 Love Languages, The 30 Day Love Detox** and **It's Just a F****ing Date**. I started reformatting how I viewed dating and relationships. I tested out "strategies" from the books. I continued to flop around like a beached whale in the dating world saying stupid things or putting too many expectations again on relationships, but I started to learn to trust in my gut properly. I started to learn to ease up on expectations and hold men to a higher standard.

My final recommendation for a book that found me just at the right time was **You Are A Badass** by Jen Sincero. This book was straight up no-nonsense truth and continued to help shape the beliefs that were building in my head. I don't think there is a perfect journey through self-development books. I love so many for so many different reasons. I think we get to fumble through life like a baby calf learning to walk, which is a beautiful part of our journey. For me, quotes and self-development books were maps and flashlights that helped guide me as I found a new path I was meant to take in life.

Here's your next journal section. Self-reflection is different for everyone, dive into these questions or save them to the end. There is no manual for this stuff, but I'm hoping these questions help you organize your thoughts no matter where you are in your journey.

SELF-DEVELOPMENT JOURNAL SECTION

1. *What quotes stood out to you?*

2. *What did that quote or quotes mean to you?*

3. *What does self-help or self-development mean to you?*

4. *How does the term self-love resonate with you?*

5. Is self-forgiveness easy or hard for you?

6. Make a list of books that you want to dive into.

[7]

Bucket Lists

PAINFUL MEMORIES from a past relationship with a significant other can ebb and flow through the mind. The good and the bad can come in waves. When dark moments were stuck inside my brain I was lost in a web of insomnia and grief. Pinterest quotes and therapy only helped so much. I would go to work, call my girlfriends, call my mother, go to therapy sessions, and just try to keep my head above water. To start living again, I needed to get back to doing things and discovering new things that I enjoyed before entering into this relationship, as well as finding new things that I could incorporate into my life. After establishing self-care and healthy habits that kept me afloat during immense grief portions of my healing journey, I also wanted to start figuring out what lit me up inside before I met my ex. I also wanted to learn new things about myself as I emerged a different person on the other side of grief.

I recognized that I gave up truly living an amazing life while I was in the relationship. I can look back and see the things I gave up in my attempts to make another person happy. I stopped going to the gym so I could be home to make him happy. I stopped eating healthy so I could cook his meals to ensure he was eating nutritiously. I was also emotionally eating my weight in worry and frustration. I thought that if I did everything in my power to make someone else happy, then they would be happy. I had no understanding of the personal concept of happiness until after I left the relationship. I had no concept that we choose our own happiness. I didn't understand that no matter what I did I couldn't make another person happy, especially someone who was so deeply unhappy with themselves. I forgot about the airplane oxygen-mask theory. If the oxygen mask drops in an airplane we are told we must put the mask on ourselves first before helping another person. I had no concept that I needed to fill my cup before I could pour it into his. I notice to this day that I have a very hard time being around negative people or those that focus on the worries in their life. Because I've done so much self-love work it's a trigger for me and I have to distance myself from them, whether it's limiting conversations or hiding Facebook posts.

To focus on happy and fun I decided to start small. I went back to my habit of creating short-term and long-term goals. I started with my health first. I got excited about creating weekly meal plans and grocery shopping lists again. I

knew I had to feel healthy again to help my brain in its healing process. So one week I set a goal to get back to eating
five to six healthy meals a day. The second week I ensured
that I was consuming two to three liters of water a day. The
third week I got into the gym three times. Then the fourth
week I went to the gym four times and the next week five
times. My routine gave me structure, purpose, and kept my
brain focused on the task at hand: just feeling healthy
again. Since I had gained several unhealthy pounds from
emotional eating and lack of exercise, and I knew I needed
to feel like myself again, I focused on my nutrition, exercise, and water consumption.

Once the happy hormones from health and fitness were
running through me, I started dating again. The man (mentioned in my Happiness Journey chapter) that was placed in
my life taught me what I needed at that moment in time. I
discovered that I love adventure, fun, and creating moments in my life that truly make me feel alive. On top of
introducing me to obstacle course races, he was an adrenaline junkie, a traveler, and a bucket list completer. I saw
something in him that I yearned for in my life. I am thankful for my time spent with him and know why he was placed
in my path. I adopted new physical challenges into my life,
so I could push myself further than I had in the past. From
2009 – 2011 I was defining myself as a fitness competitor. I
trained hard in the gym, got dolled up, and pranced around
on stage in a bikini. I had completed a physical challenge
and become stronger by training, but I hadn't shown the

world how strong I was at this point. I also wasn't challenging myself to see how strong I could really become. On my goal spreadsheet that I complete every January, I started dreaming big in my goals for the upcoming 2013 year. In 2012, I ran the Warrior Dash mud run, which proved I could complete an obstacle course; however I didn't know if I could run three races in one year. I was introduced to the world of Tough Mudder by the guy I dated, so I planned to run my first Mudder in May of 2013. I planned on running Warrior Dash, Tough Mudder, and Mud Hero that year to see what my body could do. Little did I know that would then lead me to complete six obstacle course races in 2014 and then tackle twenty races in 2015.

I had found a new physical challenge for my fitness goals for the year. I was back on track with my nutrition and feeling healthy again. My job and advertising career were keeping me busy during the day, but I wanted to feel like I was living my life again. I quickly wanted to discover activities that would bring me joy.

I found inspiration in the reality show star Lauren Conrad and a fitness duo I admire, the Tone It Up girls. They were posting on their websites about Summer Bucket Lists. I hadn't really thought about seasonal bucket lists to make the most out of Canada's four short but sweet seasons. So I created my first Summer Bucket List and had an amazing first summer as a single woman. I started by listing things that I thought would be fun. I copied some of the ideas from Lauren and the TIU girls. As I completed all of the items on my list, my heart started filling with joy. Some items that were not completed were moved to my list for the following summer.

When winter started looming on the horizon and I realized gloomy weather was around the corner I created a Winter Bucket List. All of a sudden the winter started to look exciting. I created my lists thinking of who I could do each item with, as well as things on the list that I could check off all on my own. A lot of the items that find themselves on my bucket lists are things I've never tried or things that I love. I truly believe trying something for the first time and accomplishing it is an addictive happy high that I love experiencing.

Here are my 2013, 2014 and 2015 Summer Bucket Lists so you can see how I became more adventurous every year as I developed the adrenaline junkie lover in me. After I discover something that I love, I also try and ensure that I keep it in my life by putting it on a seasonal bucket list the next year.

2013
Make Kabobs on the BBQ
Healthy Picnic
Warrior Dash Mud Run
Cottage Weekend
Mud Hero Mud Run

5K Color Run
10km Night Race
Fitness Competition
Canoe Trip
Drive In Movie
Golf
Balcony Garden
Random Road Trip

2014
Bicycle Wine Tour
Stand Up Paddleboard Yoga
Kite Boarding
Ocean Kayaking
Random Road Trip
Golf
Drive In Movie
Balcony Garden
Picnic
Stargaze on a Dock
Sail
Wakeboarding
Wakesurfing
Camping
Caving
Outdoor Concert
Street Food Festival
CN Tower Edgewalk
North Face 10K Trail Race

Spartan Obstacle Course Race
Warrior Dash Mud Run
Tough Mudder Mud Run
X Man Obstacle Course Race
Dead End Obstacle Course Race
5 Peaks Trail Races (5 Trail Races)

2015
Skydiving
Bungee Jumping
Ziplining
Tree Trekking
Balcony Garden
Canoe Trip
Kite Boarding
Stand Up Paddleboard Yoga
Night Stand Up Paddleboarding
Stargaze on a Dock
Wakeboarding
Wakesurfing
Caving
Outdoor Rock Climbing
Golf
Canada's Wonderland
Yoga Camp
Spartan Obstacle Course Race Trifecta (Run the Sprint, Super & Beast Distance in One Year)
Tough Mudder Mud Run
X Man Obstacle Course Race

Dead End Apocalypse Obstacle Course Race
Battlefrog Obstacle Course Race
Nike 15K Road Race

Now sit back for a moment. Close your eyes and think about the smile that spreads over your face after you accomplish something for the first time. That moment and feeling is priceless and almost indescribable. Let me help you picture it a bit more. When you were a kid, do you remember how proud you were when you stood up for the first time and took your first steps? Probably not, but I bet you your parents can remember the grin that spread across your face. Think back to the first time you tied your shoes, saw an animal at the zoo, rode a bike, hit a baseball or wore your first party dress. Let the feeling of accomplishment and pride wash over you for a second and picture that feeling. Over the years I stopped thinking like a kid. I stopped thinking about all the fun things I could try in life. I forgot what it was like to adventure. As I started to do new things for the first time in my adult life I was able to recreate those feelings. My healthy addiction to completing things on my seasonal bucket lists bring me the best warm fuzzy feelings - the ones that spread from your heart throughout your body.

In addition to creating warm fuzzies for myself, bucket lists were important for me to regain my sense of self. When I created the commandment "Be Robyn," what did Robyn stand for? What did Robyn enjoy? What were things

I could call my hobbies and pastimes? I also realized bucket lists became important tools as I developed new relationships while dating and growing friendships.

I have this love affair with romantic comedies. We could also psycho-analyze how that maybe created the wrong type of expectations in my romantic relationships, but let's save that for another book *wink wink*. I realized as I was creating seasonal bucket lists that I was creating moments in my life that I wanted to photograph or capture on film. I call these movie moments. A movie moment to me is where the couple or friends are perfectly in frame, as he takes her on an adventure or the group of friends goes on a random road trip. In a romantic relationship the camera zooms in, there is a pause, time stand stills, the audience holds their breath in anticipation, they wish for the moment to happen, and boom he kisses her. In a group of friends, the camera view is from above, capturing the windswept hair of the group of friends as they jump in a convertible and hit the road for a girls' weekend of adventuring, and it captures everyone smiling and laughing perfectly.

I wanted to build a life, as I learned to love myself again, that was worthy of a movie camera following me around. Sometimes the memory of a bucket list item would be captured on my smart phone in the form of a picture and other times they would just happen and I only have a mental picture to remember the moment by. When I incorporated firsts and movie moments into my life I felt more alive. I felt like I was truly living and taking advantage of all the time I do have on this planet. I also felt like I was creating moments that allowed for a greater connection with others.

As I started dating again, I embraced being the Alpha Female that I am with the adventurer and life seeker sides to me. Why not date and try new things at the same time? I really don't like the standard coffee or dinner date. It feels too much like an interview, and to be honest it's tiring going on a ton of first dates and talking about yourself over and over again no matter how much you love yourself. So I would create fun lists of things I'd like to do on dates and or share my bucket list with potential first dates. It's one of the reasons why I found myself doing the CN Tower edge walk, going snowmobiling, going bouldering at a rock climbing gym or snowshoeing through a vineyard on first dates. Although the men weren't right for me, I have amazing memories of the adventure we tried and started seeing dating as a positive thing in my life versus a draining, tiring, despairing or annoying thing that single people have to do.

I also realized that I was counteracting not having any recollection of positive memories with my ex. So while I have this need to create a perfect life, I was fulfilling that need by doing everything in my power to create a great life and great memories in a healthier way. I never tried to force movie moments, but definitely set the scene so they could potentially happen. It's also helped me embrace spontaneity and find other people who embrace fun. I've sipped tea in the trunk of a jeep backed up over an outlook. I've sat on a lifeguard chair at the Scarborough bluffs listening to music and swimming in the rain. I've stargazed on a dock talking for hours. I've gone winter camping (which I never would've considered) and sat by a campfire and lit sparklers at midnight.

As I set the scene for romantic movie moments in my life, I also started creating ones in my friendships. I soon realized as friends start asking what's on the bucket list that this wasn't just something I could do on my own or on dates. I started dating my friends and creating amazing memories that grew our friendships. I organized New Year's Eve and Valentine's Day brunches with my girl-friends. I organized cottage weekends with new groups of friends that I met training for obstacle course races. I jumped at the chance to go on race weekends with the people I train with, and signed up for random adventures with them. I started realizing that movie moments don't have to be romantic. They've been amazing starting points for the growth of great friendships. It's becoming a regular thing when planning a weekend for someone in the group to turn to me and ask is there anything on the bucket list we can do? It may have been the cheesy romantic comedy that inspired me, but I'm so thankful that I've been able to create, make, and have amazing movie moments in my life with so many different people. I truly believe it's one of the major reasons why I can announce from rooftops that I'm living a life that I truly love now.

Here are some questions for you to help start your own bucket list if you feel drawn!

BUCKET LIST JOURNAL SECTION

1. What experiences have you had that you miss doing in your life?

2. What are some things you want to try for the first time?

3. Do you want to push your comfort zones and try things that scare you?

4. What things can you put on a bucket list that you can do on your own?

5. What things can you put on your list that you can do with friends?

6. What things can you put on your list that you can suggest to potential dates?

[8]

Trusting Your Gut & Truths

HAVE YOU EVER MET someone and felt your body giving off negative signals? Has someone you're dating or a friend told you something and your stomach informed you whether it was the truth or not? I dived into self-help books to try to understand this reaction. I cannot explain why this phenomenon exists, but I have learned to trust when my body tells me something is wrong. I have had to learn to understand trusting my gut the hard way. Every time my gut fired in past relationships, I thought I was being paranoid. In reality, it's the wisdom from many past experiences warning me that I've already learned this lesson. I need to trust my bank of knowledge as it manifests in bodily reactions.

I knew that my relationship with my ex-fiancé was not good. I knew that things were happening behind my back, as I shared in the warning signs chapter. I chose to ignore all the signs so that I could create this image of what I thought a perfect life should be. I focused on the perfect-life picture and not the gut-wrenching feelings I had in the pit of my stomach every night. I knew in the depths of my soul how long he had been cheating on me, even though I was only given that information the month after we had parted ways.

You may have read the warning signs chapter and thought, "How dumb were you?" Sure. Hindsight or viewing it as a third party usually does that. But in the moment I was trying to be a really cool girlfriend and fiancée that wasn't controlling or questioning the time spent with friends. I didn't want to be the nagging significant other who demanded to know his every move. I wanted to trust him and show him that I trusted him. But without fail, every time I went to bed at 9pm and he still hadn't come home by 4am my stomach was in knots and I would wake up in a panic. Most nights I would be so sick in the pit of my stomach I developed insomnia. I was living in an environment ridden with anxiety.

As I began dating after leaving the relationship, I came across all different kinds of men. I made so many mistakes with these new dating experiences that I finally realized I still didn't trust my gut.

For example, two years after the break up I met a great guy that promised me the world. He was very forward with his words and said things like, "I can't wait to spend the rest of my life with you." This was said within the first two weeks of knowing me. I started questioning the words saying, "Is this too good to be true?" Although it was amazing to feel loved and wanted, I knew it was too good to be true. I knew deep down I was being lied to again. I was listening to the things I wanted to hear because I thought, "finally I've met a great man who treats me right and sees a future with me." After a month I started feeling icky - that pit-of-stomach feeling like you might vomit at any moment. I trusted my gut and did a bit of digging on Instagram (it didn't take long) and found out he was seeing another woman at the same time. I ended it immediately.

Although dating and being hurt and experiencing feelings of rejection or realizing someone isn't right for you is a hard process, I can truly say that it allowed me to really truly learn to trust my gut again. It's not a science. There is no manual. I will never be an expert, by any means, but I am a firm advocate and believer in learning to recognize that pit-of-the-stomach feeling that is trying to tell you what's going on. Whether it's your inner guide or God punching you in the stomach or your body recognizing something that doesn't seem right, that feeling should be trusted.

Other than not knowing how to trust myself as I started dating again, I was actually really terrified. I hadn't gone on a date in four years. I was hurting inside, emotional, and a bit of a train wreck. I was in many ways dating immediately after the relationship fell apart for a purpose. I was still having the thoughts, "I'm 30, I should be married and starting a family by now," running through my head. The thoughts, "I'm fabulous and gorgeous and well established; I should have no trouble finding a man as fast as possible," were also present. Even though I was posting quotes about how nothing you go through is a waste of time, I couldn't help but feel I had just wasted four years of my life and needed to get a step up on dating as soon as possible. I'm an Alpha Female after all; I should be able to attack the task of dating just like I attack projects at work. So despite knowing that I wanted to find a partner with whom I could create a family, I was also embarrassed about wanting this. I had to work through knowing what my truth is before I could embrace it.

The standard question when I started dating again seemed to be, "What are you looking for?" This seemed like such a loaded question, but I was answering truthfully that I wanted to get married and start a family someday. However, I was always so hesitant with my answer. It's as if I was embarrassed to state this truth about myself. After trying to create the image of a "perfect" life with an imperfect man, I felt guilty for still wanting those hopes and dreams. And that guilt was reflected in how I carried myself and answered dating questions. No wonder in the first two years after calling off the wedding none of my relationships survived. I was emitting fear and guilt in everything that I said and how I carried myself. I was riddled with anxiety and projecting that into the world.

I also thought I needed to tell my story about the storm in my life right away to everyone I met. I wanted them to know what I was dealing with in the back of my head. For some they appeared to respect my need to share and for others it was overwhelming. As time passed I kept the story to myself, and to this day I don't always talk about it. I'm very careful now with whom I share these private revelations. I needed time to heal. What I also needed was time to process all the thoughts associated with a healing journey. No matter how many people told me time would heal all wounds I wasn't going to understand that in the midst of my grief. I had to allow time to pass for myself. I also had to allow my thoughts to be less filled with turmoil and more filled with understanding. I found a quote early in the healing process that said, "Everyone comes with baggage. Find someone who loves you enough to help you unpack". So I jumped into the dating world with the thought in the back of my head, "I will find someone who will help me unpack." I was all gung ho about showing them the baggage right away and asking them to sign up for the unpacking immediately. I thought I was being honest with my wants and needs, but I've learned that my wants and needs are just that, mine. I was being overly vulnerable before I had even connected with them as a person. It was all about me and less about building a relationship.

I remember going on dates with what I thought was a positive attitude, but hearing so many stories from the men I was dating about women over 30 who are just baby crazy and that's all they are focused on. It was discouraging knowing it was one of my truths. Men talked about this fact with such disdain that you couldn't help but then adopt the same disdain, even though you privately yearned for this for yourself. Men would also sound so annoyed about divorced women and state they were so damaged. I wasn't divorced, but a broken heart and leaving a relationship are all devastating. I decided to take a break from dating to work on myself and my own thoughts instead of focusing on others. I learned to reframe my negative thoughts and let go of any timeline I had put in place self consciously or unconsciously. I was up against a societal view that men are scared of a woman in her 30s who is listening to her biological clock and acknowledging that she's ready to have a family and wants that for her life.

One of the dating books I dived into changed my perspective on owning my truth. I read 30 Day Love Detox by Wendy Walsh and finally started to embrace the fact that I want to be a mother and have a family someday. This desire is something to be proud of rather than scared of. However, I still wasn't very good at communicating this sentiment. I still remember going on one date with a comparatively younger man. I don't know why I decided to bring up my truth in his car on a random drive and ended up crying, while revealing I couldn't wait to be a mom and have kids. I know I was crying because it saddened me that we weren't in sync with our hopes and dreams. He told me I was the most emotional person he'd ever dated. I can look back at that moment and smile and recognize why I was being "so emotional" about it. I was still healing. I was still hurt. The poor guy had no idea that I had all this pent up hurt and was so scared to even admit to a man that this is something that I want. He got a Robyn full of fear instead of Robyn who is certain and strong in her truths. Once I started calmly accepting that this is my truth and releasing the fear, I began speaking authentically without emotion. That is when men started to embrace it and respect it, even if it wasn't something they shared. I also realized that, when I shared my truth with someone and I didn't end up being emotional about it, I felt support in sharing my dreams.

Dating is very much like going on a job interview. If you don't think you'll get it, you won't. I was so scared they were going to call me a typical baby-crazy 30-year-old that I made jokes about it to hide my insecurity. One of my favourite quotes from the movie The Perks of Being a Wallflower is: "We accept the love we think we deserve". I was accepting going on dates with men that I believed would find my desire repulsive and so it manifested as truth. I kept accepting the love I thought I deserved versus what I really deserved. I had to flip my way of thinking to: "I deserve a man that adores me and shares in my truth."

When it comes to accepting and wanting our truths I had to learn to be proud of them. I want to be married to one man. I want to be a mom. I was trying to force my life into a timeline that I had planned, while the universe and God taught me that I couldn't control my timelines. I learned to set aside timelines for now. With the reality of age and childbearing, I am embracing my truth and I own it now. I've learned not to throw it out immediately in a relationship to truly get to know someone without the thought of timelines. One of the most positive relationships I've been in allowed me to truly learn this. I dated a great man in 2015. It was the longest relationship I'd been in since calling off the wedding. I didn't mention wanting children until six months into our relationship. I still didn't know how to approach telling someone this is my truth, but I knew that I had to share it for the relationship to potentially grow into something more. I still shared my truth awkwardly and was slightly emotional again. I know it's because I already recognized that it wasn't his truth.

I believe we don't share our truths or things that we want in life in the same way as others. It's uniquely ours to own and learn. It's something deep down that we need to embrace for ourselves. In our own unique way we learn to be proud of our truths and how to communicate them without fear. I've realized it's going to look so different for everyone and that's why I couldn't actually pick up a book or read a quote to tell me how to do it myself. I was going to have to stumble through life a bit until I met someone with whom I could share my truth, not feel any trepidation about it, and stand in confidence.

I know for a fact that we are all empowered to teach ourselves self-love, compassion, and forgiveness. We are all empowered to spend time in contemplation, to learn to trust our gut in every situation, and just be ourselves.

So as I continue on my happiness journey I'm just going to be Robyn: An Alpha Female, strong, passionate, cute, awkward, ungraceful, blurting out words at the wrong times. I'm going to be adventurous, introverted, and caring. I'm going to be ambitious, but strive for amazing relationships in all aspects of my life. I can't wait to see where it takes me.

Where is your adventure going to lead you?

Here are some questions for you to start asking yourself if you know how to trust your gut or to start identifying how. These journaling questions will also help you define your truths to help guide your life as you move forward.

GUT & TRUTH JOURNAL SECTION

1. Describe what your "gut" feeling feels like in your body.

2. What are your truths? What are things you want for you life?

3. How do you want to live your life?

4. Describe how it would feel to share your truth with someone who shared the same values.

[9]

Closing Thoughts

Am I leading a life that I love? I can answer this question easily, with a resounding YES! Is my life miraculously perfect after a few years of healing? No, but I'm quite fine with that. I don't believe you can snap your fingers and just move through grief in an instant. I believe we all process grief and sadness differently, and I believe we need to be kinder to ourselves as we work through emotions. I have learned that we need to make space for ourselves to be in sadness first and then ask ourselves, "How can we grow from here?" I needed to accept grief before I could embrace amazing moments in my life and then build from there. I learned this concept the hard way by continuing to believe that I was a strong Alpha Female who didn't need to feel any sadness. I held onto a belief that I was supposed to be stronger than the sad feelings that were coming up. That belief pattern led to bottled up emotions and many breakdowns over the years at inopportune times when memories would surface unexpectantly.

I hadn't really thought about writing a conclusion to this book because that seems so finite. This journey is far from over. My healing and happiness journey I believe will always continue. There is no destination in mind other than continually loving myself, always learning to speak my truth, trusting my gut, and finding daily a life that I love.

However, since the purpose for sharing a picture into my life is to inspire hope, I'm excited to announce that at the time of this publication I'm in a loving relationship. Prior to this, I found myself in a relationship that was built on friendship first. Although we didn't share the same truths or family values or goals, we spent an amazing year together. We filled our days with adventure and great conversation and we were able to complete the relationship and move forward in a healthy and honest way. I've now met the man I want to build a life with. It is amazing how your heart becomes calm when you meet someone whose values and goals match yours. He cherishes the same family values as I do and openly communicates these things. We're building a home together and our own little family unit. We already have our own little brood that includes two fur babies.

I share this information simply because at this moment in time, as I sit down to my computer to type, I'm filled with love. I'm grateful and hopeful for my future, but working hard every day to just be more present in every moment. I'm trying my best to be less obsessed with timelines and filled with gratitude for the day. I've built and am building a life that I absolutely love, and I wish this for anyone that has ever had their heart broken from a relationship that engulfed them. I believe you can find yourself again.

References

BOOKS

Baldwin, Robyn, How to Live Like an Alpha Female, (ebook, 2012).

_____, Live Like an Alpha Female, (update, pdf, 2015).

Behrendt, Greg, and Amira Ruotola, I's Just a F***ing Date, (Diversion, 2013).

Bernstein, Gabrielle, Add More Ing to Your Life, a hip guide to happiness, (Harmony, 2011).

_____, May Cause Miracles, a 40-day guidebook of subtle shifts for radical change and unlimited happiness, (Harmony, 2014).

_____, Miracles Now, 108 life-changing tools for less stress, more flow, amd finding your true purpose, (Hay House, 2014).

_____, Spirit Junkie, a radical road to self-love and miracles, (Harmony, 2012).

Chapman, Gary, The 5 Love Languages, the secret to love that lasts, (Moody, 2014).

Greenberger, Dennis, PhD, and Christine A. Padesky, PhD, Mind Over Mood, change how you feel by changing the way you think, (Guilford Press, 1995).

Rubin, Gretchen, The Happiness Project, (Harper Collins, 2012).

Sincero, Jen, You Are a Badass, how to stop doubting your greatness and start living an awesome life, (Running Press, 2013).

Tolle, Eckhart, The Power of Now, a guide to spiritual enlightenment, (New World Library, 2004).

Walsh, Wendy, The 30-Day Love Detox, cleanse yourself of bad boys, cheaters, and men who won't commit—and find a real relationship, (Rodale, 2013).

MOVIES

Free Willy (1993).

Legally Blonde (2001)

The Perks of Being a Wallflower (2012)

What Women Want (2000)

TELEVISION DRAMAS

Sex and the City (1998-2004)

WEBSITES

LaurenConrad.com

GretchenRubin.com

LoveTinyDevotions.com

PsychologyToday.com

RobynBaldwin.com

ToneItUp.com

ABOUT THE AUTHOR

Robyn Baldwin is an Alpha Female and a Work / Life Harmony Strategist. She is a Marketing Manager, a fitness/lifestyle blogger at RobynBaldwin.com, a former CFL cheerleader and fitness competitor, a published fitness model, a freelance writer, a brand ambassador, a sponsored athlete and a podcaster. With a passion for fitness Robyn loves running, weight lifting, spin and yoga. She now spends the majority of her spare time training for obstacle course racing. She also calls herself an MS Warrior after being diagnosed with Multiple Sclerosis in December of 2014.

Made in the USA
Middletown, DE
16 August 2018